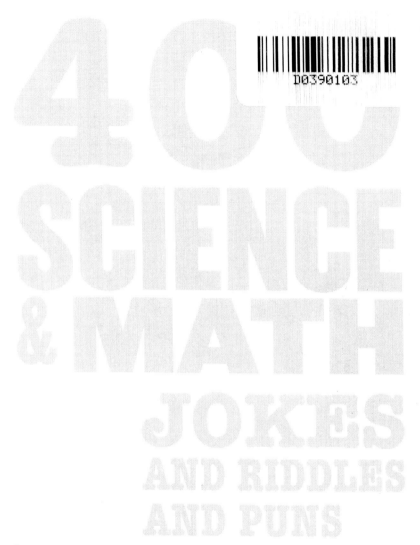

# 400 SCIENCE & MATH JOKES AND RIDDLES AND PUNS

AQUILINE

NEW YORK

# 400

# SCIENCE & MATH

## JOKES
### AND RIDDLES
### AND PUNS

COMPILED BY

# HANK McROY

ISBN-13: 978-1543117912
ISBN-10: 1543117910

**AQUILINE**

A publication of Aquiline Books

Printed in the United States of America

10 9 8 7 6 5 4 3 2 1

# 400
## SCIENCE
## & MATH
### JOKES
### AND RIDDLES
### AND PUNS

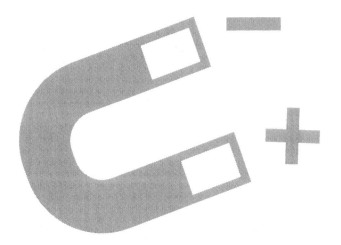

1 A group of mathematical functions are having a party. Everyone is having fun, except for $e^x$, who is standing alone in the corner.

The party host walks up to $e^x$ and says, "Have some fun! Integrate!"

$e^x$ replies, "That won't change anything...."

2 **I asked the guy sitting next to me if he had any Sodium Hypobromite...**

He said, "NaBrO."

3 Silver walks up to Gold in a bar and says, "AU, get outta here!"

4 **Why did Chlorine's sisters Boron and Carbon lock her in the closet?**

Because she was too attractive!

5 **What sound does a drowning analytic number theorist make?**

Log log log log...

**6  Which books are the hardest to force yourself to read through?**

Friction books.

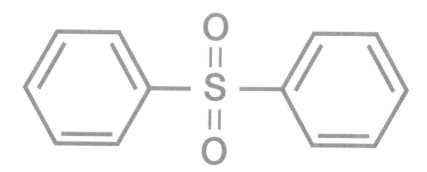

**7  How do Sulfur and Oxygen communicate?**

A sulfone.

**8**  A logician's wife is having a baby. The doctor immediately hands the newborn to the dad. His wife asks impatiently: "So, is it a boy or a girl?" The logician replies, "Yes."

**9  Did you hear about the constipated mathematician?**

He worked it out with a pencil.

**10** An anesthesiologist is flying across the country for a conference, when a flight attendant comes running down the aisle, shouting, "Is anyone on board an anesthesiologist?"

The anesthesiologist raises his hand, and asks whether anyone is sick.

"Oh, no one's sick, but there's a surgeon up in first class who needs his table adjusted."

**11 Why was the mole of oxygen molecules excited when she walked out of the singles bar?**

She got Avogadro's number!

**12 A cop pulls Heisenberg over and asks him, "Do you know how fast you were going?"**

Heisenberg replies, "No, but I know where I am."

**13 How did the chemist survive the famine?**
By subsisting on titrations.

**14** A British mathematician was giving a talk in Grothendieck's seminar in Paris. He started, "Let X be a variety...".

This caused some talking among the students sitting in the back, who were asking each other, "What's a variety?"

J.-P. Serre, sitting in the front row, turns around a bit annoyed and says, "Integral scheme of finite type over a field".

**15** Florence Flask was getting ready for the opera. All of a sudden, she screamed, "Erlenmeyer, my joules! Somebody has stolen my joules!"

The husband replied, "Calm down; we'll find a solution."

**16** **$H_2O$ is water and $H_2O_2$ is hydrogen peroxide. What is $H_2O_4$?**

Drinking, bathing, swimming, etc.

**17** **What is the fastest liquid on Earth?**

Milk. It's pasteurized before you even see it.

**18** **What do you call a FISH with no eyes?**

A FSH.

**19** Velociraptor $= \dfrac{\text{Distraptor}}{\text{Timeraptor}}$

**20** A physicist, a biologist, and a mathematician are observing a house. First they watch two people go inside, and a few moments later, three people come out.

The physcist proclaims, "Our knowledge of the problem is incomplete."

The biologist argues, "They reproduced!"

The mathematician concludes: "If only one more person will go in now, the house will be empty."

**21** **What did the electrical engineer say when he got shocked?**

That hertz.

**22**  **There were four houses on a street.**
**The red house was made out of brick.**
**The purple house was made out of brick.**
**The yellow house was made out of brick.**

What was the greenhouse made out of?

**23**  **What does the B in "Benoît B. Mandelbrot" stand for?**

Benoît B. Mandelbrot.

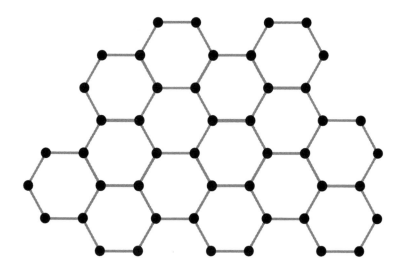

**24**  **A superconductor walks into a bar.**
**The bartender says, "We don't serve your kind around here."**

The superconductor leaves without putting up any resistance.

**25** **What's the most musical part of a chicken?**
The drumstick.

**26** **What is it called when Queen of England passes wind?**
A noble gas.

**27** **Why aren't computer scientists allowed to landscape?**
They keep planting the trees upside down.

**28** **There are two types of people in the world.**
Those who can extrapolate
from incomplete data.

**29** **Why do programmers always mix up Christmas and Halloween?**
Because OCT31==DEC25

**30** **Why wasn't the spiral galaxy allowed into the nightclub?**
He had previously been barred.

**31**  **A man walks into the doctor's office with a carrot in his nose.**

The doctor says, "I don't think you're eating properly."

**32**  Anions aren't negative; they're just misunderstood.

**33**  **How much room is needed for fungi to grow?**

As mushroom as possible.

**34**  **What do you get when you cut an avocado into 6.02 x 10^23 pieces?**

Guacamole.

**35** **A couple of biologists had twins.**

They named one Jessica
and the other Control.

**36** If you're not part of the solution,
you're part of the precipitate.

**37** **How many biologists does it take
to change a light bulb?**

Four. One to change it and three to write
the environmental impact statement.

**38** **What do you call a veterinarian
that only works on one species?**

A doctor.

**39** **What do you get when you cross a
mosquito with a mountain climber?**

Nothing. You can't cross
a vector with a scaler.

**40** **I have a question about the workers
at the chemical plant.**

Are they unionized?

**41** **What do you call the leader of a biology gang?**

The nucleus.

**42** # Let $\varepsilon < 0$

**43** **Why did the algae join with the fungus?**

They took a lichen to each other.

**44** **Why can't you grow wheat in Z mod 6?**

Because Z mod 6 isn't a field.

**45** When you breathe, you inspire.

When you do not breathe, you expire.

**46** **A man tells his doctor, "I need your help, I've broken my arm in two places!"**

The doctor replies,
"Don't go to those places!"

**47** Home is where your displacement is zero.

**48**
Dear mRNA,

I'm sorry I kept inserting tyrosines when you were, in fact, repeatedly asking me to stop.

Sincerely, Amber

**49** **Anyone can build a bridge.**

It takes an engineer to *just barely* build a bridge.

**50** Two neutrinos go through a bar...

**51** **What is the chemical formula for "coffee"?**

CoFe2

**52** When a programmer goes to bed, she sets out 2 glasses on his bedside table: one glass is full of water, in case she wants to get a drink; one glass is empty, in case she doesn't.

**53** Plateaus are the highest form of flattery.

**54** My astronomy professor told me I was his star pupil.

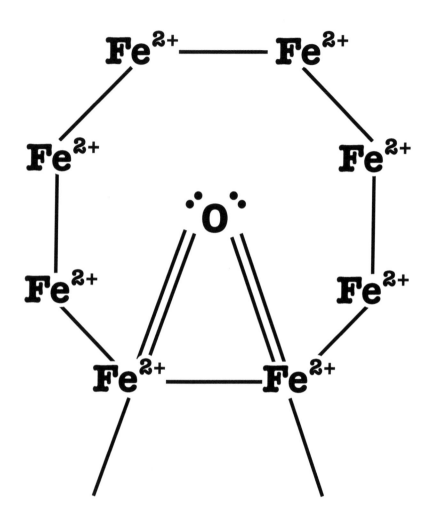

**55** **What do chemists call a benzene ring with iron atoms replacing the carbon atoms?**

A ferrous wheel.

**56** What kind of work do you do?

"Oh, I work with kidneys."

"So do you work in nephrology or pediatric orthopedics?"

**57** **Why did the engineer cross the road?**

Because he looked up what to do in a table and that's what they did last year.

**58** Two chemists go into a bar. The first one said "I think I'll have an $H_2O$."

The second one said, "I think I'll have an $H_2O$ too." And then he died.

**59** **Did you just mutate for a stop codon?**

Because you're talking nonsense!

**60** The name's Bond. Ionic Bond.
Taken, not shared.

**61** **Why did the bee go to the doctor?**

Because he had hives.

**62** **Why can't you hear a pterodactyl go to the bathroom?**

The p is silent.

**63** **What's purple and commutes?**

An abelian grape.

**64** **What kind of notebook does a dendrochronologist use?**

A tree-ring binder.

**65** **If athletes get "athlete's foot," what do astronauts get?**

Missile toe.

**66** **What do you call a dinosaur who is elected to Congress?**

Rep. Tile!

**67** **What did the hipster dog say to his owner?**

My favorite frequency is 50,000 hertz but you've probably never heard of that.

**68** **Where do elephants live after high school?**
The pachydorm.

**69** A proton and a neutron are walking down the street.
The proton says, "Wait, I lost an electron."
The neutron says "Are you sure?"
The proton replies, "I'm positive."

**70** **How do astronomers see in the dark?**
They use standard candles.

**71** Biology is the only science in which multiplication is the same thing as division.

**72** An engineer, a physicist and a mathematician check into the same hotel, but in different rooms. While they are sleeping, a fire breaks out in the engineer's room and spreads to the other two rooms.

The engineer wakes up, gets some water and douses the flames.

The physicist wakes up, calculates exactly how much water is required to put out the fire, retrieves that much water and puts out the fire.

The mathematician wakes up, thinks for a moment as he stares at the fire, exclaims, "Eureka! A solution exists!" and goes back to sleep.

**73** **What do moon people do when they get married?**

They go on their honeyearth!

**74** Science can tell you how to clone a Tyrannosaurus rex.

Humanities can tell you this is a bad idea.

**75** New engineer: "How do you estimate how long a project will take?"

Seasoned engineer: "I add up the time required for each task, then multiply the sum by pi."

New engineer: "Why pi?"

Seasoned engineer: "It ensures that all my budgets are irrational."

**76** **Online currency has recently been discovered to be a not-yet-identified super heavy element.**

The proposed name is: Unobtainium.

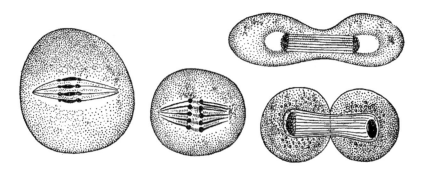

**77** **We have to stop talking about mitosis...**

It's such a divisive issue.

**78** **What did the subatomic particle say to the duck?**

"Quark, quark"

**79** **What is the chemical formula for the molecules in candy?**

Carbon-Holmium-Cobalt-Lanthanum-Tellurium

**80** **What do you think of that new restaurant on the moon?**

The food's great but it has no atmosphere.

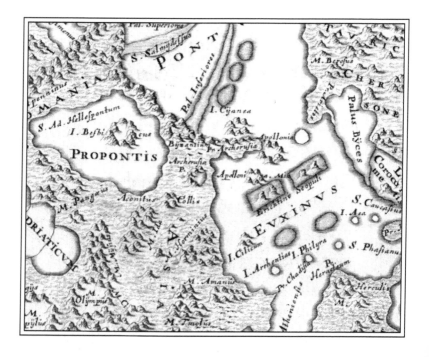

**81** **Why do hummingbirds hum?**

Because they don't know the words.

**82** **What is the easiest way to determine the sex of a chromosome?**

Pull down its genes.

**83** If you want to understand recursion, you need to understand recursion first.

**84** Time flies like an arrow.

Fruit flies like a banana.

**85** Two combinatorics professors are standing on a farm. The first professor says, "I wonder how many cows there are in this field."

The second professor proclaims, "Two hundred."

The first says, "Wow, how did you know that?"

The second says, "I counted the legs and divided by four."

**86** **I chose to become a dermatologist.**

I thought about it really carefully;
it wasn't a rash decision.

**87** Werner Heisenberg's epitaph reads,
"He lies here, somewhere."

**88** **What is the difference between
mechanical engineers and civil engineers?**

Mechanical engineers build weapons.
Civil engineers build targets.

**89** A biologist, a physicist, and a chemist
go to the beach.

The biologist decides he'd like to study
the plants at the bottom of the lake,
so he jumps in.

The physicist wants to measure the
oscillating properties of the waves,
so he jumps in.

When neither of them returns after some
time, the chemist concludes that biologists
and physicists are water soluble.

**90** "You're so hot you denature my
proteins."

**91** **Why did the chicken walk down the Möbius strip?**

To get to the other side.

**92** It's appropriate that online identity thieves are in the business of stealing ones and zeros....

**93** **Why did the electron throw up?**

He was spinning.

**94**  **Why can't you tell jokes in base 8?**

Because seven ten eleven.

**95**  When the programmer was leaving work at the end of the day, his wife called him and said, "On the way home, stop by the food store. Get a gallon of milk, and if they have eggs, get a dozen."

The programmer comes home with thirteen gallons of milk.

His wife asks, "Why did you buy so much milk?"

The programmer says, "They had eggs."

**96**  **Why can you never trust atoms?**

They make up everything!

**97**  **How did the herpetologist know he would be married soon?**

He caught the garter snake.

**98** Customer: "Do you have any two-watt, 4-volt bulbs?"

Sales Rep: "For what?"

Customer: "No, two."

Sales Rep: "Two what?"

Customer: "Yes."

Sales Rep: "No."

**99 How many mathematicians does it take to change a lightbulb?**

One; he gives the lightbulb to three engineers, thus reducing the problem to a previously solved joke.

**100 I wish I was adenine.**

Then I could get paired with U.

**101 What is the first derivative of a cow?**

Prime Rib!

**102 What are environmentally conscientious European physicists called?**

Con-CERN-ed.

**103** **One physicist asks another physicist, "What's new?"**

E over H.

**104** To the person who invented zero: thanks for nothing.

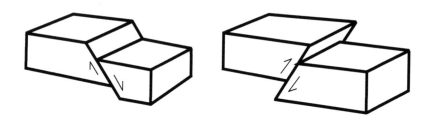

**105** Tectonic relationship:

A: There's too much friction between us!

B: It's not my fault!

**106** **How many clowns can you fit in a car?**

As many as you want; they're Bozons!

**107** **How would you skin Schroedinger's cat?**

Using an inverse furry transform.

**108** **How did carbon propose to Hydrogen?**

With a "carbonkneel."

**109** **What do you call a periodic table with gold missing?**

Au revoir

**110** René Descartes enters a bar.

The bartender asks "Do you think you'd like a beer?"

Descartes responds, "I think not," and he disappears.

**111** **What do you call a tooth in a glass of water?**

One molar solution.

**112** **Can a kangaroo jump higher than the Empire State Building?**

Of course. The Empire State Building can't jump.

**113** **Did you hear oxygen and magnesium got together?**

OMg!

**114** **Why are Math books sad?**

Because they are full of problems.

**115** An infinite number of mathematicians walk into a bar.

The first one says, "I'll have a pint."

"Half a pint for me, please" says the second one.

The third one requests, "Quarter of a pint, please," and so on and so on.

After five minutes, the bartender puts two pints on the bar and says, "You guys need to learn your limits."

**116** A parasite walks into a bar.

The bartender says, "Get out! We don't serve parasites here!"

The parasite replies, "Well, you're not a very good host!"

**117** **What did the dinosaur say when he saw the volcano explode?**

What a lavaly day!

**118** **Why was the scuba diver failing Biology?**

Because he was below "C" level.

**119** The ungulate says to the parasite, "You make me sick so I am going to expel you. You can't stay with me anymore."

To which the parasite replies: "But I encyst!"

**120 Why do chemists like nitrates so much?**

They're cheaper than day rates.

**121 How does Juliet maintain a constant body temperature?**

Romeostasis.

**122 What does an astronomer blow with gum?**

Hubbles.

**123** Helium walks into a bar.

The bartender says, "We don't serve noble gasses in here."

He doesn't react.

**124** First Law of Thermodynamics: You can't win. Second Law of Thermodynamics: You can't break even. Third Law of Thermodynamics: You can't stop playing.

**125** $e_x$ was walking down the street one day and met a polynomial running in the opposite direction. "Why are you running?" asked $e_x$.

The polynomial said, "There's a differential operator over there! It could differentiate me and turn me into zero!" And the polynomial continued running in fright.

"Ha ha," $e_x$ said to himself. "I'm $e_x$! Let them differentiate me as many times as they want, it makes no difference to me!" So $e_x$ walked on and reached the differential operator. He confidently introduced himself: "Hi, I'm $e_x$!" The reply:

"Hi, I'm $\partial/\partial y$!"

**126** **What do you call a student that got C's all the way through medical school?**

Hopefully not your doctor.

**127** **Why was the Calculus teacher bad at baseball?**

He was better at fitting curves than hitting them.

**128** **Why did the engineering students leave class early?**

They were getting a little ANSI.

**129** **Why do you never hear the number 288 on television?**

It's two gross.

**130** **Why did the noble gas cry?**

Because all his friends argon.

**131** **Why won't P and X live in the suburbs?**

Because they don't commute.

**132** **What did the Mass Spectrometer say to the Gas Chromatograph?**

Breaking up is hard to do.

**133** A little boy refused to run anymore. When his mother asked him why, he replied, "I heard that the faster you go, the shorter you become."

**134** **Is the symbol for silicon the same in Spanish?**

Sí.

**135** If the Silver Surfer and Iron Man team up, they'd be alloys.

**136** Sherlock Holmes and Dr. Watson are on a camping trip. They pitch their tent and lay down to sleep. In the middle of the night, Holmes wakes up and says, "Watson, wake up; look up at the stars, and tell me what you see."

Watson replies, "I see millions and millions of stars."

Holmes says, "What can you deduce from that?"

Watson pauses for a moment, and says, "If there are millions of stars, and even if only a few of them have planets like Earth, then there must be life out there."

Holmes, exclaims, "Watson, it means somebody stole our tent!"

**137** **What kind of fish is only made of atoms of sodium?**

2 Na

**138** **How did the hipster chemist get burned?**

He touched the beaker before it was cool.

**139** **What kind of songs do the planets like to sing?**

Neptunes.

**140  Why couldn't the angle get a loan?**

His parents wouldn't cosine.

**141  What do you give a sick bird?**

Tweetment.

**142  What did one quantum physicist say when he wanted to fight another quantum physicist?**

Let me atom!

**143**  I tried walking up a hill without a watch, but had neither the time nor the inclination.

**144**  Little Willie was a chemist.
Little Willie is no more.
What he thought was $H_2O$ was $H_2SO_4$.

**145** **Why was the cowboy bad at math?**

Because he always rounded up!

**146** **How do you tell an extroverted mathematican from an introverted one?**

An extroverted mathematician stares at *your* shoes when talking to you.

**147** May the **m × a** be with you.

**148** **What's the difference between a general practitioner and a specialist?**

One treats what you have, the other thinks you have what he treats.

**149** **What's wrong with getting flowers?**

Well, they have a certain stigma about them.

**150** Normal people believe that "if it ain't broke, don't fix it."

Engineers believe that "if it ain't broke, it doesn't have enough features yet."

**151** **How can you spot a chemist in the restroom?**

They wash their hands before they go.

**152** **What did the cowboy chemist tell his horse?**

HIO Ag!

**153** **What's wrong with a joke involving Cobalt, Radon, and Ytterium?**

It's CoRn Y.

**154** At the end of a job interview, a human resources manager asks the young engineer, "What starting salary are you looking for?" The engineer says, "Somewhere around $100,000 per year, depending on the benefits package."

The manager says, "Well, what do you say to a package of $200,000 per year, six weeks vacation, 2 weeks of paid holidays, full medical and dental insurance, 50% retirement fund matching, and a company car?"

The engineer exclaims, "That sounds great! Are you joking?"

The manager responds, "Sure, but you started it."

**155** **Did you hear about the man who got cooled to absolute zero?**

He's OK now.

**156** **What element is a girl's future best friend?**

Carbon.

**157** **If H2O is the formula for water, what is the formula for ice?**

H2O cubed.

**158** **What did one ion say to the other?**

I've got my ion you.

**159** **What is the name of the first electricity detective?**

Sherlock Ohms

**160** **Why does hamburger yield lower energy than steak?**

Because it's in the ground state.

**161** **What do you call a faulty spirometer?**

Expired.

**162** **What is hallucinogenic and exists for every group with order divisible by p^k?**

A psilocybin p-subgroup.

**163** **What happens when spectroscopists are idle?**

They turn from notating nuclear spins to notating unclear puns.

**164** **What do you call cabs which provide drug therapy?**

Chemotaxis.

**165** **Did you know oxygen went on a date with potassium?**

It went OK.

**166** **Have you heard the one about a chemist who was reading a book about helium?**

He just couldn't put it down. It was very uplifting.

**167** They have just found the gene for shyness. They would have found it earlier, but it was hiding behind two other genes.

**168** **Organic chemistry is difficult.**

Those who study it have alkynes of trouble.

**169** A patient goes to a doctor.
The doctor gives him six months to live.

The patient couldn't pay his bill, so the doctor gave him another six months.

**170** **What do philosophical dolphin say?**

"What's the porpoise?"

**171** A: "What is the integral of 1/cabin?"

B: "log cabin."

A: "Nope, houseboat—you forgot the C."

**172** **What is the chemical formula for "banana"?**

$BaNa^2$

**173** **How can you tell if there's an elephant in the refrigerator?**

The door won't close.

**174** There's a fine line between numerator and denominator.

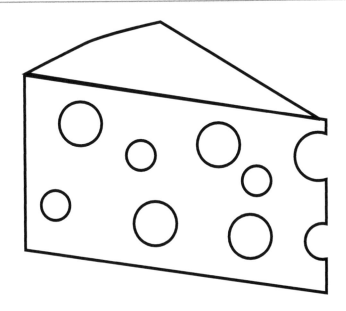

**175** Swiss cheese has holes. The more cheese you have, the more holes you have. The more holes you have, the less cheese you have. Therefore, the more cheese you have, the less cheese you have.

**176** **Old MacDonald had a farm**

minus e-squared o

**177** **Why are chemists great for solving problems?**

They have all the solutions.

**178**

"Hi, I'd like to hear a TCP joke."

"Hello, would you like to hear a TCP joke?"

"Yes, I'd like to hear a TCP joke."

"OK, I'll tell you a TCP joke."

"Are you ready to hear a TCP joke?"

"Yes, I am ready to hear a TCP joke."

"Ok, I am about to send the TCP joke. It will last 10 seconds, it has two characters, it does not have a setting, it ends with a punchline."

"Ok, I am ready to get your TCP joke that will last 10 seconds, has two characters, does not have an explicit setting, and ends with a punchline."

"I'm sorry, your connection has timed out. Hello, would you like to hear a TCP joke?"

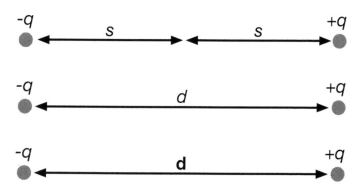

**179**

**What do dipoles say in passing?**

Have you got a moment?

**180** A man in a hot air balloon realizes he is lost. He lowers his altitude and sees a woman standing on the ground below. He asks her, "Can you help me? I was supposed to meet a friend an hour ago, but I don't know where I am."

She answers, "You're in a hot air balloon hovering 25 feet above the ground. You're between 40° and 41° north latitude and between 75° and 76° west latitude.

"You must be an engineer," says the baloonist.

"How did you know?" she replies.

"Well," the man says, "everything you've told me is technically correct, but I don't know what to do with that information, and I'm still lost. You haven't been much help, and if anything, you've delayed my trip."

"You must be in management," she says.

"Yes," replies the baloonist. "How did you know?" The woman answers, "You don't know where you are or where you're going." You have risen to where you are mostly because of hot air. You made a promise which you have no idea how to keep, and you expect the people below you to solve your problems. The fact is, you are in exactly the same position you were before me met, but now, somehow, it's my fault."

**181** **What's worse than finding a worm in your apple?**

Finding half of a worm.

**182** **Why is the Rational Root Theorem so polite?**

It minds its p's and q's.

**183** **Why did the student get upset when his teacher called him average?**

It was a mean thing to say!

**184** **What's the difference between an auto mechanic and a quantum mechanic?**

The quantum mechanic can get the car inside the garage without opening the door.

**185** **What do you call a place of worship made out of amino acids?**

A cysteine chapel.

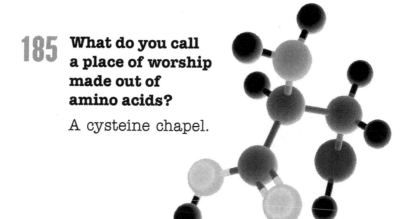

**186** **Two antennas got married.**

The wedding was lousy,
but the reception was outstanding.

**187** Seen on the door to a light-wave lab:

**CAUTION! Do not look into laser
with remaining eye.**

**188** Q: "Doctor, before you performed the autopsy, did you check for a pulse?"

A: "No."

Q: "Did you check for blood pressure?"

A: "No."

Q: "Did you check for breathing?"

A: "No."

Q: "So, then it is possible that the patient was alive when you began the autopsy?"

A: "No."

O: "How can you be so sure, Doctor?"

A: "Because his brain was sitting on my desk in a jar."

Q: "But could the patient have still been alive nevertheless?"

A: "It is possible that he could have been alive and practicing law somewhere."

**189** I had to make these bad chemistry jokes because all the good ones Argon.

**190** **Have you ever heard the story about the germ?**

No? Never mind. It will get around.

**191** **What's non-orientable and similar to a banana?**

The real projective plantain.

**192** **Did you hear about the mathematician who's afraid of negative numbers?**

He will stop at nothing to avoid them.

**193** **What do give your favorite electrical engineer for a birthday gift?**

Shorts.

**194** **Why did the sun not go to college?**

Because it already had three million degrees!

**195** After suffering weak gain at the poles, the National Transistor Party has been trying to energize their base.

**196** **Did you hear the one about the recycling triplets?**

Their names are Polly, Ethel, and Ian.

**197** **What kind of ghosts haunt chemists?**

Methylated spirits.

**198** **What happens when electrons lose their energy?**

They get Bohr'ed.

**199** **What do you do with a sick chemist?**

If you can't helium, and you can't curium, then you might as well barium.

**200** **What do you call an elephant at the South Pole?**

Lost.

**201** **A red blood cell walked into a busy restaurant. The host asked, "Would you like to sit at the bar?"**

The red cell replied, "No, thanks, I'll just circulate."

**202** **How does our solar system hold up its pants?**

With an asteroid belt.

**203** **What was the name of the first satellite to orbit the Earth?**

The Moon.

**204** **Why do dinosaurs eat their food raw?**

Because they don't know how to cook.

**205** Classification of mathematical problems as linear and nonlinear is like classification of the Universe as bananas and non-bananas.

**206** Einstein-Pitagoras equation:

**$E = m(a\char`\^2 + b\char`\^2)$**

**207** Chemistry is physics without thought. Mathematics is physics without purpose.

**208** **What did one uranium-238 nucleus say to the other?**

Gotta split!

**209** A conclusion is the part where you got tired of thinking.

**210** **What is the name of 007's Eskimo cousin?**

Polar Bond.

**211** **What do you call a clown who's in jail?**

A silicon.

**212**  **Thanks for explaining the word "many" to me.**

It means a lot.

**213**  **How did the English major define microtome on his biology exam?**

An itsy bitsy book.

**214**  **What is green and homeomorphic to the open unit interval?**

The real lime.

**215**  **What's yellow, normed, and complete?**

A Bananach space.

**216**  **What punctuation mark can be found on the human body?**

The colon.

**217**  Why do noses run but feet smell?

**218**  **What is the show cesium and iodine love watching together?**

CsI

**219**  **Does an apple a day keep the doctor away?**
Yes, but only if you aim it well enough.

**220**  **What do you call root beer in a square glass?**
Beer.

**221**  **What's the difference between a dog and a marine biologist?**
One wags a tail and the other tags a whale.

**222**  **Why did the chemist resole his shoes with silicone rubber?**
To reduce his carbon footprint.

**223**  **A million neutrinos walk into a bar.**
One says, "Ouch."

**224**  **What do you call an Atom when it dies?**
A diatom.

**225** **What is the most important rule in chemistry?**

Never lick the spoon!

**226** **Why didn't the Romans find algebra very challenging?**

Because $x$ was always 10.

**227** **One day a policeman saw a child crying, and asked, "What's the matter?"**

The child replied, "Something that has weight and volume and occupies space."

**228** **Why do plants hate math?**

Because it gives them square roots.

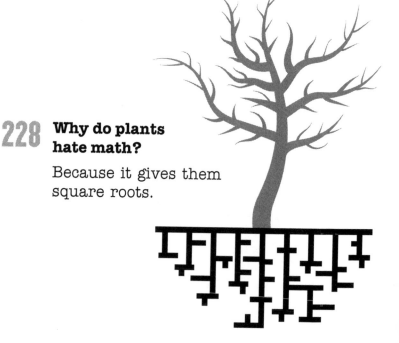

**229**  A fellow accidentally ingested some alpha-L-glucose and discovered that he had no ill effect.

Apparently he was ambidextrose.

**230**  **What's the difference between a diameter and a radius?**

A radius.

**231**  **Why do bears have fur coats?**

Because they look silly wearing jackets.

**232**  **What's big, grey, and proves the uncountability of the reals?**

Cantor's diagonal elephant.

**233**  **My friend got an A+ on his geology test.**

I told him, "Gneiss!"

**234**  **What's the best part about telling a UDP joke?**

I don't care if you get it or not.

**235** **One kid asks another,
"Which is closer, Florida or the Moon?"**

The second kid says, "The Moon, obviously;
you can't see Florida from here!"

**236** **Where does bad light end up?**

In prism.

**237** **Did you hear about the famous
microbiologist who visited 30 different
countries and spoke 6 languages?**

He was a man of many cultures.

**238** "You know, my physics teacher was
right about the optical Doppler effect.
Do you see those cars? The lights of
the cars approaching us are white,
but the lights of the cars moving
away from us are red."

**239** **Why does a moon rock taste better
than an Earth rock?**

It's a little meteor.

**240** **How many general-relativity theoretists does it take to change a light bulb?**

Two. One to hold the bulb
and one to rotate the universe.

**241** **How many ears does Captain Kirk have?**

Three. A left ear, a right ear, and a final
front ear.

**242** **Heard about that new band called 1023 MB?**

They haven't had any gigs yet.

**243** **There are 10 types of people in this world.**

Those who understand binary,
and those who don't.

**244** **What's yellow and imaginary?**

The square-root of negative banana.

**245** **What stomata with plant jokes?**

It doesn't matter.
I'm never leafing them alone.

**246** **Q: How do you catch a unique bird?**

A: Unique up on it.

**Q: How do you catch a tame bird?**

A: The tame way, unique up on it!

**247** **Why couldn't the Möbius strip
enroll at the school?**

They required an orientation.

**248** **Why was the mushroom so popular?**

He was such a fungi.

**249** A mathematician organizes a raffle,
where the prize is an infinite amount of
money paid over an infinite amount of
time. With a prize like that, he sells a lot
of tickets.

When the winning ticket is drawn, the
winner comes to claim his prize. The
mathematician says, "Congratulations!
I'll pay you one dollar today, 1/2 dollar
next week, 1/4 dollar the third week...".

**250**   **A Dirac function buys a candy bar.**

It was an impulse decision.

**251**   **What kind of plates do they use in space?**

Flying saucers.

**252**   **A pirate captain says to his first mate, "Smitty can you give me a couple of moments?"**

The first mate replies "I, I, captain!"

**253**   **What did the zero say to the eight?**

Nice belt.

**254**   **What did the bartender say when oxygen, hydrogen, sulfur, sodium, and phosphorous walked into his bar?**

OH SNaP!

**255**   **What do you call a dog magician?**

A labracadabrador.

**256** **How does the man in the moon cut his hair?**
Eclipse it.

**257** Anything that doesn't matter has no mass.

**258** **Why can't lawyers do NMR?**
Bar magnets have poor homogeneity.

**259** **How do you organize a space party?**
You planet!

**260** **How do you solve any equation?**
Multiply both sides by zero.

**261** **How many physicists does it take to change a light bulb?**
Eleven. One to do it and ten to co-author the paper.

**262** **What two elements do sheep belt when happy?**
BaH

**263** **How do you make two donuts from one?**

Through midoughsis.

**264** A mathematician, a physicist, and an engineer are building a pen in which to hold sheep, but they only have 200 feet of fencing.

The engineer gets up first, makes a square with 50 feet of fencing on each side, and proclaims, "That should work."

The physicist, says, "There's a better way...". He makes the fencing into a circle, explaining how it encapsulates the greatest possible area for the given perimeter.

The mathematician counters, "No, there's an even better way...". He tears off three feet of fencing, encircles it around himself, and says, "I declare myself to be on the outside."

**265** **What element is derived from a Norse god?**

Thorium.

**266** **Why are environmentalists bad at playing cards?**

They like to avoid the flush.

**267** Did you know that you can cool yourself to -273.15°C and still be Ok?

**268** **Why did the obtuse angle go to the beach?**
Because it was over 90 degrees.

**269** **Why did the statistician drown while crossing the river?**
It was 3 feet deep...on average.

**270** **Why did the acid go to the gym?**
To become a buffer solution!

**271** **Doctor, Doctor! I feel like a pair of curtains.**

Pull yourself together!

**272** A cowboy brings the cows back
to the shed and tells the farmer,
"All 30 cows are back."

The farmer says, "There are only 27 here."

The cowboy says, "Yes, I rounded them up."

**273** **Why did Carbon marry Hydrogen?**

They bonded well from
the minute they met.

**274** I threw a huge mitosis party
for all of my friends, but they all
just showed up, then split.

**275** **Two random variables were talking
in a bar.**

They thought they were being discrete
but I heard their chatter continuously.

**276** **Did you hear about the company
that sells elastomeric insulators?**

Their motto is "Resistance is butyl."

**277** **Old chemists never die.**

They just stop reacting.

**278** **What did the limestone say to the geologist?**

Don't take me for granite!

**279** **What's the difference between astronomy and gastronomy?**

Astronomy is about things too big
to wrap your head around,
while gastronomy is about things small
enough to wrap your head around.

**280** **Why did the leopard wear a striped shirt?**

So he wouldn't be spotted.

**281** **What is a dinosaur's least favorite reindeer?**

Comet.

**282** **Who knows everything there is to be known about vector analysis?**

The Oracle of del phi!

**283  Can you name 10 dinosaurs in 10 seconds?**

Yes. 8 Iguanadons and 2 Stegasaurus.

**284**  A small piece of sodium that lived in a test tube fell in love with a Bunsen burner. "Oh Bunsen, my flame," the sodium pined. "I melt whenever I see you."

The Bunsen burner replied, "It's just a phase you're going through."

**285  What did one titration say to the other?**

Let's meet at the endpoint.

**286  What should you do if you see a green alien?**

Wait until it's ripe!

**287  What's an anagram of Banach-Tarski?**

Banach-Tarski Banach-Tarski.

**288  What do you get if you cross Santa Claus with a space ship?**

A "u f ho-ho-ho!"

**289** It's election day. A man comes up to a statistician and says, "Aren't you going to go vote?"

The statistician says, "I'm not going to bother. The laws of probability say the chances of my vote being the deciding vote are extremely small, so it's not worth the effort."

The man says, "Oh yeah, and what if everyone is as smart as you?"

The statistician replies, "Well, the laws of probability...".

**290** **I asked a geologist how she liked her new job at the quarry.**

She said it's the pits.

**291** **I'm going to take a class on becoming an apiarist.**

At the very least I'll get a B.

**292** **Where do they send the criminal neurons?**

To the chain ganglion.

**293** **Why didn't the Dog Star laugh at the joke?**

It was too Sirius.

**294** **Why do bees have sticky hair?**

Because they have honeycombs.

**295** **What did the man say to the x-ray technician after swallowing some money?**

"Do you see any change in me?"

**296** **Why did the polynomial plant die?**

Its roots were imaginary.

**297** Philosophy is a game with objectives and no rules.

Mathematics is a game with rules and no objectives.

**298** The optimist sees the glass half full.
The pessimist sees the glass half empty.

The chemist sees the glass completely full, half in the liquid state and half in the vapor state.

**299** **What did one cell say to his sister cell when she stepped in his toe?**

Mitosis!

**300** A mechanical engineer, a chemical engineer, an electrical engineer, and a computer engineer are all riding in a car. The car breaks down.

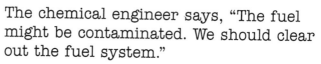

The mechanical engineer says, "I think the pistons have seized. We'll have to tear apart the engine and rebuild it."

The chemical engineer says, "The fuel might be contaminated. We should clear out the fuel system."

The electrical engineer says, "It might be a wiring problem, or a bad spark plug."

The computer engineer says, "Maybe we should all get out of the car and get back in again?"

**301** **How many forensic scientists does it take to change a light bulb?**

Two. One to screw in the bulb, and one to check for fingerprints.

**302** **How many programmers does it take to change a light bulb?**

None. It's a hardware problem.

**303** **What did one flea say to the other flea when they came out of the movie theater?**

"Should we walk home or take a dog?"

**304** **One plant says to the other, "Are you hungry?"**

The other replies,
"I could use a light snack".

**305** A math student gets back to her house at 3AM, and gets yelled at by her parents.

"You're late!" they exclaim. "You said you'd be home by 11:45!"

She replies, "Actually, I said I'd be home by a quarter of twelve."

**306** The optimist sees the glass as half full.

The pessimist sees it as half empty.

The engineer sees it as twice as large as it needs to be.

**307** Professor: "5,000 feet! That's over 50 atmospheres of pressure!

Student: How many atmospheres can the ship withstand, professor?"

Professor: "Well, it's a spaceship. I'd say somewhere between zero and one."

**308** **Why shouldn't you argue with a decimal?**
Decimals always have a point.

**309** **How is the moon like a dollar?**
Because it has four quarters.

**310** **What kind of accident is closed under join?**
An up-set.

**311** **What do you call an alien with three eyes?**
An aliiien.

**312** Two blood cells met and married.
Alas, it was all in vein.

**313** It's not the $V_f = V_i + at$ that kills you,
it's the $F = m(\Delta V / \Delta T)$.

**314**    **A photon checks into a hotel and is asked if he needs any help with his luggage.**

He says, "No, I'm traveling light."

**315**    **There is a rooster sitting on a top of a barn. If it laid an egg, which way would it roll?**

Roosters don't lay eggs!

**316**    **What happened to the man who was stopped for having sodium chloride and a nine-volt in his car?**

He was booked for a salt and battery.

**317**    **What do physicists enjoy doing most at sporting events?**

The wave.

**318**    A student riding in a train looks up and sees Einstein sitting next to him. Excited, he asks, "Excuse me, professor: does Boston stop at this train?"

**319**    Pavlov is sitting in his house. The phone rings. He jumps up and shouts, "Time to feed the dog!"

**320** **Have you heard the latest statistics joke?**
Probably.

**321** **What do you call an educated tube?**
A graduated cylinder.

**322** **Why didn't Sine cross the road?**
Cosecant.

**323** A neutron walks into a bar. He asks the bartender, "How much for a beer?"

The bartender smiles and says, "For you, no charge".

**324** **What is a pirate's favorite amino acid?**
AAAARRRRRRginine.

**What is a pirate's favorite nucleic acid?**
AAAARRRRRRNA.

**What is a pirate's favorite element?**
Gold.

**325** The goal of science is to build better mousetraps.

The goal of nature is to build better mice.

**326** A statistician is someone who tells you that, when you've got your head in the fridge and your feet in the oven, you are, on average, very comfortable.

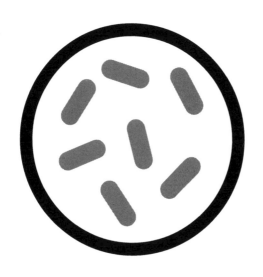

**327** A bacteriologist is a man whose conversation always starts with the germ of an idea.

**328** **What did the male stamen say to the female pistil?**

I like your "style."

**329** **Why does 0 have such a hard time finding a job?**

It doesn't have a degree.

**330** A blowfly goes into a bar and asks: "Is that stool taken?"

**331** Have you heard that entropy isn't what it used to be?

**332 Why do chemists enjoy working with ammonia?**

Because it's pretty basic stuff.

**333 I was up all night wondering where the sun had gone....**

Then it dawned on me.

**334 The first mathematician asks, "So, why did you become a mathematician?"**

The second mathematician replies, "I don't like working with numbers."

**335 Why did the poultry farmer become a schoolteacher?**

So he could grade his eggs.

**336 Where did Gauss keep his cows?**

In the magnetic field!

**337 How does the nucleus communicate with ribosomes?**

With a cell phone.

**338 What is non-orientable and lives in the ocean?**

Möbius Dick.

**339 A teacher with strabismus was fired.**

She could not keep her pupils straight.

**340** One day, Einstein, Newton, and Pascal meet up and decide to play a game of hide and seek. Einstein volunteered to be "It." As Einstein counted, eyes closed, to 100, Pascal ran away and hid, but Newton stood right in front of Einstein and drew a one meter by one meter square on the floor around himself.

When Einstein opened his eyes, he immediately saw Newton and said, "I found you Newton." Newton replied, "No, you found Pascal!"

**341 What did one sister chromatid say to the other?**

"Stop copying me!"

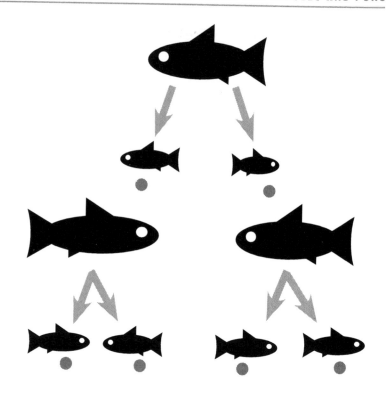

**342** **What is a nuclear physicist's favorite meal?**

Fission Chips.

**343** Einstein developed a theory about space. And, it was about time, too.

**344** **What do organic mathematicians throw into their fireplaces?**

Natural logs.

**345**  **There are 10 types of people in the world.**

Those who understand ternary,
those who don't, and those that thought
this was going to be a binary joke.

**346**  **What did the conservative biologist say?**

The only cleavage I want to see
is at the cellular level.

**347**  **Why does it take a million sperm to fertilize one egg?**

Because none of them will ask
for directions.

**348**  **What is a cation afraid of?**

Dogions.

**349**  **What do you do if you see an aggressive alien?**

Give it some space!

**350**  **What did Gregor Mendel say when he founded genetics?**

Woopea!

**351** An experimental physicist meets a mathematician in a bar, and asks, "What kind of math do you do?"

The mathematician replies, "Knot theory."

The physicist says, "Me neither!"

**352** **Why did Fermat write his proof in the butter?**

Because there wasn't enough room in the margarine.

**353** **What do you call a grizzly bear caught in the rain?**

A drizzly bear.

**354** **What did the femur say to the patella?**

I kneed you.

**355** **What do you call a number that can't keep still?**

A roamin' numeral.

**356** **What did the scientist say when he found 2 isotopes of helium?**

HeHe

**357** **How many astronomers does it take to change a light bulb?**

None; astronomers prefer the dark.

**358** **Professor: "Give an example of a vector space."**

Student: "V"

**359** **The bartender says, "We don't serve faster-than-light particles here."**

A tachyon enters a bar.

**360** **Where do hippos take college classes?**

Hippocampus.

**361** **What kind of snake excels at mathematics?**

An adder.

**362** A bar walks into a physicist.

Oh, sorry, wrong reference frame.

**363** **Anyone know any jokes about sodium?**

Na

**364** "Today," said the professor, "I will be lecturing about the liver and spleen."

One student turns to another and says, "Rats. If there's one thing I can't stand, it's an organ recital."

**365** **When do astronauts have lunch?**

At launch time.

**366** **What's yellow and equivalent to the Axiom of Choice?**

Zorn's Lemon.

**367** Go to Halloween parties with a friend, both dressed as doctors.

Tell everyone you're a paradox.

**368**  **Y'all want to hear a Potassium joke?**

K

**369**  **I bought a book called "101 Ways Programmers Can Fool You."**

It gave me only five.

**370**  Two fermions walk into a bar. The first one orders a vodka martini with a twist. The second one exclaims, "Rats! That's what I wanted!"

**371**  The Higgs boson walks into a church. The priest says, "hey, we don't allow Higgs bosons in here!"

The Higgs boson says, "But without me, how can you have mass?"

**372**  **What is "HIJKLMNO"?**

$H_2O$.

**373**  **Have you heard about the cow astronaut?**

He landed on the moooooon!

**374**   **What did Al Gore play on his guitar?**
An Algorithm

**375**   **What's a pirate's favorite programming language?**
R, but his heart will always belong to the C.

**376**   **Why did the bear dissolve in water?**
It was polar.

**377**   **You enter the laboratory and see an experiment. How will you know which class it is?**
If it's green and wiggles, it's biology.
If it stinks, it's chemistry.
If it doesn't work, it's physics.

**378**   **How many balls of string would it take to reach the moon?**
One. A large one.

**379**   Researchers in Fairbanks, Alaska announced last week that they have discovered a superconductor which will operate at room temperature.

**380** A frog telephones the psychic hotline. His psychic advisor tells him, "You are going to meet a beautiful young girl who will want to know everything about you."

The frog is thrilled, "This is great! Will I meet her at a party?"

No, says the psychic. "In her biology class."

**381** **What animal is made up of calcium, nickel and neon?**

A CaNiNe

**382** A paramecium and an amoeba are walking down the street. The amoeba asks "So, lacking any psuedopodia, how do you manage to get around?

The paramecium replies, "A cilia question I've never heard!"

**383** **What is very old, used by farmers, and obeys the fundamental theorem of arithmetic?**

An antique tractorisation domain.

**384** A young engineer was leaving the office at 6PM when he found his boss standing in front of a shredder with a piece of paper in his hand.

"Listen," said his boss, "this is important, and my assistant has left. Can you make this thing work?"

"Certainly," said the young engineer. He turned the machine on, inserted the paper, and pressed the start button.

"Well done!" said his boss as the paper disappeared inside the machine. "I just need one copy."

**385** **What is a paramecium?**

Two latin mice.

**386** Pi and i get into an argument. Pi says, "I'm just keeping it real."

i says, "No, you're being irrational."

**387** **Teacher: "What is the definition of a protein?"**

Student: "A protein is something that is made up of mean old acids."

**388** **Why couldn't the astronaut book a room on the moon?**

Because it was full.

**389** **What washes up on beaches?**

Nucleotides.

**390** **How did the English major define microtome on his biology exam?**

An itsy bitsy book.

**391** **What do you call an illegally parked frog?**
Toad.

**392** **How do you eat DNA-spaghetti?**
With a replication fork.

**393** **How do you identify a bald eagle?**
All of his feathers are combed over
to one side.

**394** **Why did I divide sin by tan?**
Just cos

**395** **What did the chemist snack on during lunch?**

Gram crackers!

**396** **Why is electricity an ideal citizen?**

Because it conducts itself so well.

**397** Does a radioactive cat have 18 half-lives?

**398** **Why did the chicken cross the road?**

The answer is trivial and is left as an exercise for the reader.

**399** **What emotional disorder does a gas chomatograph suffer from?**

Separation anxiety.

**400** **Why did Werner Heisenberg hate driving cars?**

Every time he looked at the speedometer he got lost!

Made in the USA
San Bernardino, CA
17 October 2018